Pebble® Plus

## Celebrating Differences

# We All Have
# Different Abilities

## by Melissa Higgins

Consulting editor: Gail Saunders-Smith, PhD

Consultant: Donna Barkman
Children's Literature Specialist and Diversity Consultant
Ossining, New York

**CAPSTONE PRESS**
a capstone imprint

Pebble Plus is published by Capstone Press,
1710 Roe Crest Drive, North Mankato, Minnesota 56003.
www.capstonepub.com

 Books published by Capstone Press are manufactured with paper
containing at least 10 percent post-consumer waste.

*Library of Congress Cataloging-in-Publication Data*
Higgins, Melissa
  We all have different abilities / by Melissa Higgins.
     p. cm.—(Celebrating differences)
  Includes bibliographical references and index.
  Summary: "Simple text and full-color photos celebrate different and varied abilities"—Provided by publisher.
  ISBN 978-1-4296-7575-8 (library binding)
  ISBN 978-1-4296-7888-9 (paperback)
  1. Ability. I. Title.
  BF431.H449 2012
  153.9—dc23                                          2011040395

**Editorial Credits**
Jeni Wittrock, editor; Gene Bentdahl, designer; Svetlana Zhurkin, media researcher; Kathy McColley, production
    specialist; Marcy Morin, studio scheduler; Sarah Schuette, photo stylist

**Photo Credits**
Alamy: Jim West, 17, Photofusion Picture Library, 11, Stock Connection Distribution, 19; Capstone Studio: Karon
Dubke, 7, 9, 13; Corbis: Brian Mitchell, 5, 15, moodboard, cover; Getty Images: Don Smetzer, 1; iStockphoto:
fatihhoca, 20–21

## Note to Parents and Teachers

The Celebrating Differences series supports national social studies standards related to
individual development and identity. This book describes and illustrates different abilities. The
images support early readers in understanding the text. The repetition of words and phrases
helps early readers learn new words. This book also introduces early readers to subject-specific
vocabulary words, which are defined in the Glossary section. Early readers may need assistance
to read some words and to use the Table of Contents, Glossary, Read More, Internet Sites, and
Index sections of the book.

Printed in the United States of America in North Mankato, Minnesota.
012013    007153R

# Table of Contents

# On My Own

I can do things on my own.

At school and at home,

I am busy, busy, busy.

# I Can Get Ready

It's morning. I button my shirt
and fasten my shoes.
Head to toe, I do it
all by myself.

When I fix my own breakfast,

I don't spill a drop.

I'm proud of what I can do.

It's time for school! I can't wait
to see my friends on the bus.

11

# I Can Learn

My teacher asks a question.

I know the answer.

Pick me, teacher!

Numbers are cool. I am great at math. I help my friend with a tough problem.

# I Can Play

Here comes the ball.

THWAP!

I hit it with my bat.

Do you want to join our game?

The swings are crowded today.

I wait my turn.

WHOOSH!

It is worth the wait!

Let's have some fun!
We sing, clap, and
play songs. There are
so many things we can do.
What can you do?

# Glossary

crowded—lots of people

fasten—to bind things together

proud—feeling good about who you are and what you do

# Read More

**Bunnett, Rochelle.** *Friends at School.* New York: Star Bright Books, 2006.

**Dwight, Laura.** *We Can Do It!* New York: Star Bright Books, 2005.

**Moore-Mallinos, Jennifer.** *It's OK to Be Me!: Just Like You, I Can Do Almost Anything.* Live and Learn. Hauppauge, N.Y.: Barron's Educational Series, Inc., 2007.

# Internet Sites

FactHound offers a safe, fun way to find Internet sites related to this book. All of the sites on FactHound have been researched by our staff.

Here's all you do:

Visit *www.facthound.com*

Type in this code: 9781429675758

Super-cool stuff! Check out projects, games and lots more at **www.capstonekids.com**

# Index

Word Count: 151
Grade: 1
Early-Intervention Level: 17